SATANIC [illegible] ION

BLA[illegible] RACE

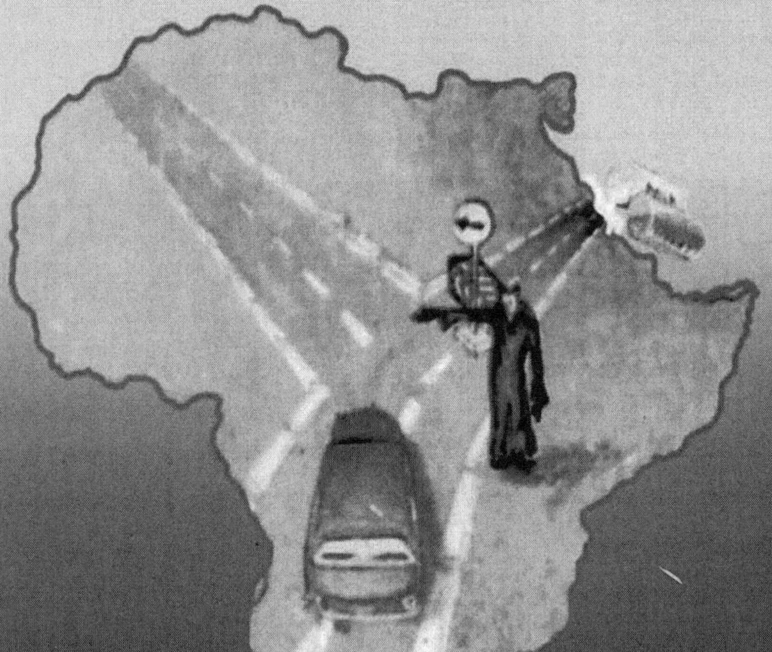

MOUNTAIN OF FIRE AND MIRACLES MINISTRIES

DR. D. K. Olukoya

SATANIC DIVERSION OF THE BLACK RACE

DR. D. K. OLUKOYA

ISBN 978-2947-15-6

A publication of
MOUNTAIN OF FIRE AND MIRACLES MINISTRIES
13, Olasimbo Street, off Olumo Road,
(By UNILAG Second Gate), Onike, Iwaya
P. O. Box 2990, Sabo, Yaba, ☎4704367 Lagos, Nigeria.
mfm@micro.com.ng mfm@nigol.net.ng
www.mountain-of-fire.com

Typesetting, Designing and Printing at
MFM PRESS
13, Olasimbo Street, off Olumo Road,
by Unilag 2nd Gate, Onike, Yaba, Lagos, Nigeria.

Cover *Illustrated by* - **Sister Shade Olukoya**

All Scriptures are quoted from the King James Version of the Bible

First Edition 1998
Second Edition 2002
Third Edition July 2010

CONTENTS

This book is designed by the Holy Ghost to change lives and situations. It is not an ordinary book. Please, say these aggressive prayer points before you start reading.

PRAYER POINTS

1. I refuse to obey any satanic instruction, in the name of Jesus.
2. I stand against every operation and activity of the spirit of death and hell, in the name of Jesus.
3. Every satanic stronghold camping against me, be roasted, in the name of Jesus.
4. Let every attack fashioned against my progress be frustrated, in the name of Jesus.
5. I paralyse every power blocking my spiritual vision, in the name of Jesus.
6. Holy Spirit, fill me with fresh fire.
7. Thank the Lord for the prayer session.

INTRODUCTION

This message is meant to enlighten our spirits and explain certain questions which might have been agitating the minds of many people.

I read Psalm 42:7:

> ***Deep calleth unto deep at the noise of thy waterspouts.***

Some of the things I am going to say in this book may be new to some people, but the idea is to put them down until they get into your individual lives.

A lot of statements have been made about Christianity by educated people, including Africans. Some tell us, that Christianity is a foreign religion, that it is something that was imported to us and they do not know why we are taking it so seriously. Others feel that it is a white man's culture. Many of these educated people argue that if you put a piece of bottle down and decide that it is your god, then it is your god. Even if it is not a piece of bottle, but a stick in your bedroom, as far as you believe that it is your god, then you can continue to worship it.

They forget the words of Scriptures in Psalm 115:4-8 which says,

> ***Their idols are silver and gold, the work of men's hands. [5]They have mouths, but they speak not: eyes have they, but they see not: [6]They have ears, but they hear not: noses have they, but they smell not: [7]They have hands, but they handle not: feet have they, but they walk not: neither speak they through their throat. [8]They that make them are like unto them; so is every one that trusteth in them.***

This is a faithful statement. Just as they are dumb and deaf, those who worship them are also deaf and dumb.

Many years ago, when I was in the University, there was a young man who argued this very verse coherently, to prove that we should go back to the dumb idols we were serving, and he convinced so many people.

This young man argued so much and tried to confine God to a test tube. However, God cannot be confined to an experiment. But something shocked me, just a few months back. I saw the brother here and asked, "My friend, what are you doing at Mountain of Fire and Miracles? Here we call upon the living God." He said, "Heaven help us." He continued that he did not come here by chance. He went to a party where he found a nice girl, and they committed immorality together but he was not satisfied and so asked if he could follow her home. He also asked the girl whether she was married and she said, "No." He then said, "Okay, let's go."

So they went to her house, and closed the door. Just as they were about to settle down and continue to enjoy their sin, there was a knock on the door. The man asked, "Who is knocking?" The woman answered, "My husband." The man said, "But you told me that you are not married." "That was a slip of tongue", said the woman. The man asked, "What can I do now?" The woman told him to hide under the bed. But the aggressive knocking was still going and the brother then hid under the bed. He was afraid at the aggression with which the man banged the door, then he thought that if a man who was banging the door like that came in and found him, only heavens would be able to help him.

So he said to the woman, "It is not too late now, can I jump out through the window?" The woman said, "Yes." So he jumped out and found himself in a cemetery. He did not know where he jumped out from; he just found himself walking around in the cemetery. He eventually walked out through the gate, and as from that time, his life was never the same again. Problems started here and there, and that was what brought him to MFM. The same Jesus that he did not want to serve is the One who delivered him:

There was also another case. When I was in the University, there used to have a lecturer, who taught us Physics. During a forty-five minute lecture, he would spend half an hour to tell the students that there is no God and fifteen minutes for Physics. Surprisingly, he was winning converts and there were people who believed him. Those who were going to church before stopped going, because of what this lecturer was teaching.

I remember a boy called Sunday who was a good boy and was regularly going to church; but after listening to this lecturer with his demonic logic, he too stopped going to church. Something happened to him one night which changed him forever. He was coming from a party around 1:00 a.m, when suddenly, out of the corner of a bush, he saw a naked man carrying a pot of sacrifice. When Sunday looked closely and saw that it was the lecturer, he called him, but the man did not answer. Sunday then regained his senses. He said to himself, "this man comes to the lecture room and says that there is no God, but here he is sorting himself out with the devil at night." That changed him.

This is the deception you sometimes find in the so-called educated people. Sometimes, you cannot blame them, because the early Pentecostal fathers cleared away the forests, the demons who were moving freely about and the evil things which were swallowing people alive. Therefore, someone can now put on a 'three-piece-suit' and say that there is no God. In those days when witches were moving about in the afternoon, you do not need to be convinced that there is God. Even if you do not believe in God, you believe that there is one evil power that can kill.

A lot of people who have been questioning about Christianity here, will find out if they go abroad, that the white man has gone back to the witchcraft which had put us in trouble.

A friend of mine was preaching in Europe and suddenly, he broke down and cried. He then said, "You people, you brought Christianity to us, you are now back to the dumb idols we were trying to reject." He then called out in the open congregation, "If you are a witch or a wizard and you are in this meeting, come out."

The pastor of the church was shocked to find white men and women trooping out to renounce witchcraft. Take a journey abroad now and in all the popular bookshops, you will find a section with books on the occult. Books on how to become a witch are not hard to find.

So a lot of these arguments go on. Why are you so interested in something that the white man brought and he is no longer interested in, that is, Christianity?

We are told all kinds of strange stories about the black man and even if they do not tell stories about the black man, there are a lot of things that you yourself can notice.

PECULIARITIES ABOUT BLACK MAN

- One out of four of the world's population lives in a state of extreme poverty.
- The richest fifth have incomes which are 60 times greater than the poorest fourth, twice the disparity of 30 years ago.
- The poorest 50 countries, mostly in Africa are homes to one-fifth of the world's people and account for less than 2 per cent of global income.
- African economies, with about 10 per cent of the world's population, account for 0.4 per cent of world manufacturing exports and less than 1 per cent of world trade.
- The extra cost of tied aid represents more than 15 per cent of the aid provided which is equal to some $4bn a year, and more than the entire UK aid budget. About $8,000 debt rescheduling took place between 1980 and 1992 in Africa alone.
- Some 35,000 children die every day, from preventable diseases.

- The greatest number of killers of black people are the black people themselves. Black against black.
- You will notice that amongst the black race, the inferior person is elevated and the superior is pulled down.
- Someone climbs up a ladder, but removes it so that no other person can climb up.
- Africa is a cemetery of wasted lives and buried potentials.
- A father knows that he has something that will help his children but will not tell them and will rather hide these things.
- The closest person to someone will be busy destroying the person in the spirit world and will be taking the same person around for assistance.
- The first person that is likely to be killed, is the person who would bring progress to the group.

Nobody needs to tell us these stories, we know them. So what exactly is wrong with the black man? Why do they tell us strange stories?

A white man cracked a very dirty joke in England and said that when God was creating the world and got to Nigeria and was putting crude oil, coal and minerals inside the ground, that some people protested, and asked, "God, why are you giving them so much?" The man continued, "God then laughed and said, 'wait until you see the kind of people I will put there, and let us see whether they can manage them or not.'"

Why are they telling these kinds of stories about us? What exactly, beloved, is wrong with the black man?

Some people said that, at a time when God created men, He had a swimming pool and wanted the men to wash themselves. When the water was clean, the white man jumped in, washed himself, and came out looking white. By this time, the water was a bit dirty. Then the Chinese jumped inside, and when he came out, he was a little bit dark. The water was dirtier. When the water was very dirty, the black man jumped inside and so became black.

Why do people make statements like these? Why do some people also say, "the average black man is stupid, organization wise?" What is the explanation for our treasures that are being misused? Why should someone bring a piece of mirror and with it, collect fifty slaves?

WHAT IS THE REASON FOR OUR DOMINATION?

Have you not noticed that the entire African Continent known as "the dark Continent" was ravaged and looted by the white man, who carried people away during the slave trade? Why did we have to go through that horrifying slave trade experience where people were packed like sardines, inside a ship? If you made the mistake of falling sick, there was no treatment; they just took the sick man and threw him into the sea. When they got to the plantation fields, they locked their mouths up with padlocks, so that they could not eat the sugar-cane. And God sat on His throne and watched all these things happening.

Why is it difficult to find a single black nation that is doing very well? Why is it that we do not contribute to most of the good things going on in the world? Why is there this demonic and diabolical attack from hell fire to stop black people from exercising their spiritual and physical mandate? Does God have a purpose for the black man at all? What exactly is God's purpose for the black people?

THE INTERVENTION OF THE WHITE MISSIONARY

The white missionaries did not help matters much. They called some names Christian names and said that others are not Christian names. *For example, Onyekachi* (an Ibo name in Nigeria) means "who is greater than God?" *Philip,* which you find in the Bible (and most people will prefer it to Onyekachi), means "a lover of horses." So, it is not your name that makes you a Christian. Christianity is not about names but about your relationship with the Lord Jesus Christ.

They also told us that there is a place called the Holy Land. The Bible does not recognise a place called the Holy Land. What the Bible recognises is this, Where two or three are gathered 'in My Name, there I will be in their midst.

Those who brought Christianity here did not really understand our spiritual environment and the strongmen in charge of the African people. Therefore, when they built their church, they did not understand how to exorcise the land, and command the demons there to flee. The land was already an altar of the enemy, now a church was built on that altar; soon, demons started to flow into the church and every top member of the church became a lodge member because the churches were built on altars and the missionaries did not understand where they were. These early churches in Africa had no fire to quench any satanic revival.

In many cases, it was just a change from one idol to another. People abandoned their local idols or still kept them at home and went after another one they called 'Mary'. The kind of demonic honour that some people are giving to Mary today is not in the Bible. In fact, Mary herself knew that she was a sinner and needed the baptism of the Holy Ghost and was also one of those who gathered in the upper room.

It is a pity that some people are defending Mary today but refuse to follow Mary to the upper room where she got on fire. And thank God she was one of those who received the baptism of the Holy Ghost and spoke with tongues. God has put us here for a purpose and that purpose is clear in the Scriptures.

WHAT IS GOD'S PURPOSE FOR THE BLACK MAN?

What is God's purpose for the black man according to the Scriptures? And what has kept the black man from fulfilling this purpose? What are the forces behind this satanic diversion? If you look through the Bible, you will find that poverty, low class accommodation and insufficient education should not only be attributed to black people all the time.

In the Bible, whenever the world has been in a crisis, God has always made a black person to appear on the scene, to show the way.

Whenever God has a major step to take in spiritual history, a black man has always come along.

SCRIPTURE REFERENCES

We are going to look at some Scriptures and I want you to ponder on their implications.

* KETURAH AND THE CHILDREN OF ABRAHAM

Abraham the father of faith, had Ishmael through Hagar, and Isaac through Sarah. What most people do not know is that Abraham still had another wife who had the highest number of children for him. He married this woman after the death of Sarah.

> ***Gen 25:1-2: Then again Abraham took a wife, and her name was Keturah. And she bare him Zimran, and Jokshan, and Medan, and Midian, and Ishbak, and Shuah.***

Keturah was from the black race. If you want to study this thoroughly, study Genesis, chapters 9 and 10.

Black people have always been around since the time of Father Abraham. Abraham signified a great change in history during the era when men began to move with God by faith. Abraham was the father of faith and did not have to import any faith for Africa separately. He had children who had strong relationships with the black race.

It is interesting to note the names of those children. The one called 'Zimran' in verse two means, 'musical'. Perhaps this is why dance and music is so natural to the Africans. The African does not need to go to the dancing school. So black people had an original and divine connection with Father Abraham. So right from that beginning, in the original programme of God, blacks have been involved.

* JETHRO, MOSES' IN-LAW

Moses was a powerful man of God. When God took him out of Egypt, it took one man called Jethro, to teach him the ways of God. Moses was the deliverer of the children of Israel from Egypt.

> ***Exodus 2:21: And Moses was content to dwell with the man: and he gave Moses Zipporah his daughter.***

The wife of Moses was Zipporah and she was an Ethiopian. If the daughter is referred to as an Ethiopian, then we know that the father too was an Ethiopian.

> ***Exodus 18:2-5: Then Jethro, Moses' father in law, took Zipporah, Moses' wife, after he had sent her back, And her two sons; of which the name of the one was Gershom; for he said, I have been an alien in a strange land: And the name of the other was Eliezer; for the God of my father, said he, was mine help, and delivered me from the sword***

> *of Pharaoh: And Jethro, Moses' father in law, came with his sons and his wife unto Moses into the wilderness, where he encamped at the mount of God:*

Bible students will recognise that Moses was attacked because of his wife. Jethro was the one who taught Moses the principles of what we call, 'division of labour in the house of God'. Moses was working so hard and was getting no-where until this man came and showed him how to divide his functions. It is therefore very strange when black people say that they cannot rule themselves. This is because there are some spiritual forces in action.

In the book of Numbers, chapter 10, you will find another black man there. When the children of Israel were going to their promised land, a black man had to come and show them the way. The name of the man was Hobab the son of Raguel. Raguel is another name for Jethro, the father-in-law of Moses.

> *Num. 10:29-32: And Moses said unto Hobab, the son of Raguel the Midianite, Moses' father in law, We are journeying unto the place of which the LORD said, I will give it you: come thou with us, and we will do thee good: for the LORD hath spoken good concerning Israel. And he said unto him, I will not go; but I will depart to mine own land, and to my kindred. And he said, Leave us not, I pray thee; forasmuch as thou knowest how we are to encamp in the wilderness, and thou mayest be to us instead of eyes. And it shall be, if thou go with us, yea, it shall be,*

that what goodness the LORD shall do unto us, the same will we do unto thee.

Eventually this man went with them, because he was asked to act as their eyes, as a scout for the people of Israel. So God's purpose is to use the black race as a spiritual eye to the nations. But where are we now? The man Hobab directed the Israelites to the promised land. So what are we trying to say? Black men have always been in the presence of God, right from the beginning. They have always been around and God had always relied on them in time of crisis.

* EBED-MELECH, THE ETHIOPIAN

Prophet Jeremiah was thrown into a dungeon when there was a serious crisis in Israel.

Jer. 38:6-13: Then took they Jeremiah, and cast him into the dungeon of Malchiah the son of Hammelech, that was in the court of the prison: and they let down Jeremiah with cords. And in the dungeon there was no water, but mire: so Jeremiah sunk in the mire. Now when Ebed-melech the Ethiopian, one of the eunuchs which was in the king's house, heard that they had put Jeremiah in the dungeon; the king then sitting in the gate of Benjamin; Ebed-melech went forth out of the king's house, and spake to the king, saying, My lord the king, these men have done evil in all that they have done to Jeremiah the prophet, whom they have cast into the

> *dungeon; and he is like to die for hunger in the place where he is: for there is no more bread in the city. Then the king commanded Ebed-melech the Ethiopian, saying, Take from hence thirty men with thee, and take up Jeremiah the prophet out of the dungeon, before he die. So Ebed-melech took the men with him, and went into the house of the king under the treasury, and took thence old cast clouts and old rotten rags, and let them down by cords into the dungeon to Jeremiah. And Ebed-melech the Ethiopian said unto Jeremiah, Put now these old cast clouts and rotten rags under thine armholes under the cords. And Jeremiah did so. So they drew up Jeremiah with cords, and took him up out of the dungeon: and Jeremiah remained in the court of the prison.*

The Lamentations of Jeremiah came from the dungeon; Ebedmelech was an Ethiopian, a black man. He came on the scene and when he did not know how to rescue Jeremiah, he tied rags together and pulled him out. A black man rescued God's prophet in the hour of need.

SUMMARY OF THE OLD TESTAMENT POSITION

Many do not know that Christianity purges all cultures. They conclude that Christianity is a white man's religion and ancestral worship is recommended as the religion of the Africans. On the contrary, Christianity is truly an African religion. It is an error to say

that Christianity is an European affair and that we should go back to our idol worship.

Idol worship is as old as the time of the fall of Adam. All nations of the world indulged in idolatry including Africans.

The Arabs used to worship "Jinns" (spirits).

Stonehenge in Southern England is a living evidence of 'Druidism', which was the heathen worship of. the early inhabitants of the United Kingdom. Human sacrifice was a part of Druid worship and was only abolished in Roman days.

While pagan worship was a part of the religion of the Philistines, the Greeks and the Romans, they could change to other religions of their choice. Why should this not be the case of Africans? The British people no longer claim 'Druidism' as their religion.

HISTORY OF CHRISTIANITY IN AFRICA

The missionaries who brought the gospel to Africa are not the first representatives of Christianity on our Continent. History actually shows that Christianity ties are closer with Africa than with Europe or North America.

The Bible presents many historical facts on the relationship of Africa with Palestine (the land of the Bible). It was out of their bondage in Africa that God redeemed His people. Egypt is a part of Africa.

> ***Princes shall come out of Egypt; Ethiopia shall soon stretch out her hands unto God (Ps. 68:31).***

Ethiopia, Egypt and Cyrene are words that are used for the continent of Africa. It is interesting to note that Africa as a continent is the most widely mentioned continent in the whole of the Bible. The prophecy in Psalm 68:31 declares that God's work would have tremendous impact in Africa in the future.

As far back as Genesis 12, God had identified with Africa. Abraham came to Africa during a famine. Abraham and Lot has so much wealth when they came into Africa and this led to quarrels between their servants.

God used Africa to support, protect and provide for His move. All the tribes of Abraham came into this continent. Joseph lived here for some time. It is thus clear that God used Africa as a ministry to provide food and shelter to prevent this vision of Israel from dying. If Joseph did not come to Africa, the whole mission about Israel would have perished. In the days of Joseph, he married an African woman and had two children.

* THE WISE MEN, SIMON - A MAN FROM CYRENE

When Jesus was born, there were some wise men who came from the East. If you do your Bible research very well, those men were black. They saw the star and followed it.

The New Testament also presents a direct link with the holy land. Jesus Christ was brought to Africa as a baby for safety from wicked king Herod.

> ***Matt. 2:15: And was there until the death of Herod: that it might be fulfilled which was spoken of the Lord by the prophet, saying, Out of Egypt have I called my son.***

Our Saviour born in Asia walked the soil of Africa.

If you go further in the Scriptures, when Jesus had been beaten up and spat on, they put the cross on Him, and when He could not carry it any more, a black man came along, to help Christ carry the cross to Calvary.

> ***Matt. 27:32-33: And as they came out, they found a man of Cyrene, Simon by name: him they compelled to bear his cross. And when they were come unto a place called Golgotha, that is to say, a place of a skull,***

The fact that a black man came along at that time is not a coincidence. He was there by divine appointment. It was this black man who carried the cross to Golgotha and this was not a coincidence. Cyrene was a town in what is now called, Libya.

* ETHIOPIAN EUNUCH

Before the gospel could reach the first European, God had to keep his covenant with the black people, by letting them hear the gospel first. The first man who caught the fire was an Ethiopian, even before it got to the first European, Cornelius.

Those of us who have studied the book of Acts, know about the

Ethiopian eunuch in Acts chapter 8. He had visited Jerusalem in an attempt to worship God and heard that there were a lot of things happening, but he did not gain anything. He was confused, and had come all the way from Ethiopia, to Jerusalem, because he wanted something. He did not get it and he was disappointed. Anyway he carried his Bible and he was reading it. The Bible they had then, was not like ours; it was a roll of leather and very heavy. Their vehicles were not comfortable like our own. This man was hungry after God, and held tight to the Scriptures he was reading in that uncomfortable situation, "As a sheep led to the slaughter . . . "

> ***Acts 8:26-38: And the angel of the Lord spake unto Philip, saying, Arise, and go toward the south unto the way that goeth down from Jerusalem unto Gaza, which is desert. And he arose and went: and behold, a man of Ethiopia, an eunuch of great authority under Candace queen of the Ethiopians, who had the charge of all her treasure, and had come to Jerusalem for to worship, Was returning, and sitting in his chariot read Esaias the prophet. Then the Spirit said unto Philip, Go near, and join thyself to this chariot. And Philip ran thither to him, and heard him read the prophet Esaias, and said, Understandest thou what thou readest? And he said, How can I, except some man should guide me? And he desired Philip that he would come up and sit with him. The place of the scripture which he read was this, He was led as a sheep to the slaughter; and like a lamb dumb before***

his shearer, so opened he not his mouth: In his humiliation his judgment was taken away: and who shall declare his generation? for his life is taken from the earth. And the eunuch answered Philip, and said, I pray thee, of whom speaketh the prophet this? of himself, or of some other man? Then Philip opened his mouth, and began at the same scripture, and preached unto him Jesus. And as they went on their way, they came unto a certain water: and the eunuch said, See, here is water; what doth hinder me to be baptized? And Philip said, If thou believest with all thine heart, thou mayest. And he answered and said, I believe that Jesus Christ is the Son of God. And he commanded the chariot to stand still: and they went down both into the water, both Philip and the eunuch; and he baptized him.

The Spirit of the Lord told Philip to join the Eunuch in his chariot. Philip asked him if he understood what he was reading, and he said, "How can I understand if there is nobody to explain." Philip then started from that portion of the Scriptures and told him about Jesus. So when the fire of Pentecost was to leave Jerusalem before it ever arrived at the door of any white man, or European, it got to the black man first through this Ethiopian. Before the Gospel reached Europe, God had to keep His covenant with the black people by letting them hear it first. So Africa got the gospel before Europe, as far as the Bible is concerned and it is there in black and white.

HISTORICAL ACCOUNTS

* FIRST MISSIONARY BIBLE

Before Christianity came, Africa knew the God of Abraham, Isaac and Jacob. As far back as around 260BC, King Ptolemy II of Egypt in Africa, established a relationship with the high priest in Jerusalem. This Egyptian ruler was interested in the Jewish way of worship. The high priest sent 6 x 12 translatable scrolls to Ptolemy's court and they translated the books of the Old Testament to Greek in 6 x 12 days. This book called the "Septuagint" or "Seventy" was accepted by the believers. This happened in Africa. ***Thus, the first Missionary Bible, was made in Egypt.***

* THE LAST EMPEROR OF ETHIOPIA

The Queen of Sheba was believed to have visited King Solomon during his reign to see his wealth and wisdom. Eventually, this woman gave birth to a son from the relationship with Solomon. The last Emperor of Ethiopia claimed that his roots were from this union between King Solomon and the Queen of Sheba. His official title was thus referred to as "Lion of Judah". The child grew up and went to his father Solomon in Israel. When returning to Ethiopia, he brought with him the greatest treasure he found in Israel; the two tablets of stone bearing the law of Moses.

* SCATTERING OF THE JEWS

The Lord ensured that in scattering the Jews, many of them established themselves throughout the near east, in Egypt, North Africa, Sudan and as far away Ethiopia. In the time of Christ, the number of Jews in Syria, Egypt and other parts of North Africa was estimated at about a million. The Jews took the holy rites along with them into these areas. The religious practice of the Ethiopian Orthodox Church today, reveals that the Ethiopians knew the Old Testament before the New Testament Gospel reached Africa. It should also be noted that the Ethiopian means "aithops", that is, "dark-skinned."

The Jews and their associates were found before the time of Christ not only in Egypt, Merve and Ethiopia, but throughout North Africa, from Alexandria to Tangiers.

> **Matt 2:12-15: And being warned of God in a dream that they should not return to Herod, they departed into their own country another way. And when they were departed, behold, the angel of the Lord appeareth to Joseph in a dream, saying, Arise, and take the young child and his mother, and flee into Egypt, and be thou there until I bring thee word: for Herod will seek the young child to destroy him. When he arose, he took the young child and his mother by night, and departed into Egypt: And was there until the death of Herod: that it might be**

> **fulfilled which was spoken of the Lord by the prophet, saying, Out of Egypt have I called my son.**

It is of utmost significance that Jesus had to be taken to Africa as a baby. The despised continent is mentioned as the place to which our Lord was taken. Again in the crisis, God turned to Africa.

* THE MARTYRDOM OF APOSTLE MARK

A ceremony which took place in Egypt in 1968 is worth mentioning. The martyrdom of Mark was commemorated. It is interesting to note and quote a section of the invitation sent out by the coptic orthodox patriarch for the ceremony.

"Shortly after the ascension of the Lord, Mark came to Egypt, he was of African descent. He was the writer of the oldest Gospel. He founded the oldest Church in Africa in Alexandria, the city which he died as a martyr in the summer of the year 68 AD."

It is not clear whether Mark is of African descent but it is significant to note that God specifically sent the writer of the oldest Gospel to Africa.

* PAUL THE APOSTLE AND HIS MISSIONARY JOURNEY

> **Acts 13:1-5: Now there were in the church that was at Antioch certain prophets and teachers; as Barnabas, and Simeon that was called Niger, and**

Lucius of Cyrene, and Manaen, which had been brought up with Herod the tetrarch, and Saul. As they ministered to the Lord, and fasted, the Holy Ghost said, Separate me Barnabas and Saul for the work whereunto I have called them. And when they had fasted and prayed, and laid their hands on them, they sent them away. So they, being sent forth by the Holy Ghost, departed unto Seleucia; and from thence they sailed to Cyprus. And when they were at Salamis, they preached the word of God in the synagogues of the Jews: and they had also John to their minister.

When it was time for Paul to be sent on his missionary journey, black men laid hands on his head and sent him forth. This may sound unbelievable to some people. There were five of them praying and the Holy Ghost said, separate unto me Paul and Barnabas for the work which I have called them. The prophecy could not have come from Paul or Barnabas. So, that leaves three people and two of these three were black. Niger and Lucius of Cyrene. They then laid hands on Paul and Barnabas and sent them out. Niger from which the river Niger and the countries of Niger and Nigeria are named means black.

So only scripturally ignorant people can maintain that Christianity is a foreign religion in Africa. The problem is that Christianity is not even a foreign culture, it is a new nature.

During the earliest period of Christianity, North Africa and Asia Minor were areas with the strongest churches. In the first four centuries, Africa produced many outstanding theologians. Augustine of Hippo has had more lasting influence on Christian theology than any other person since the Apostle Paul. His African Athanasius, Tertullian and Origen were all outstanding African theologians. To claim that Christianity is a white man's religion only because white missionaries brought the gospel two hundred years ago is not historically accurate. Christianity is an original Asian and African affair and not European affair. But this does not give an Asian or an African any monopoly on Christianity. God gave His revelation to the whole world. The invitation comes to all people of all cultures:

> ***Look unto me, and be ye saved, all the ends of the earth: for I am God, and there is none else (Isa. 45:22).***
>
> ***Come unto me, all ye that labour and are heavy laden, and I will give you rest (Matt. 11:28).***

If anyone wants to reject Christianity, he must do so on other grounds and not on the excuse that it is a white man's religion.

We are indebted to modern missionaries for bringing the gospel to Africa, but they are only messengers. Historically, Christianity was thriving in Africa long before it reached the British Isles and North America, from where so many of the Protestant missionaries came. We can, therefore, rightly call Christianity an African religion.

Several hundreds of years ago, there existed in Africa many flourishing kingdom and empires whose brand of civilization is comparable to that developed at that time in other parts of the world. These kingdoms and empires included ancient Ghana, Mali, Songhay, Hausa states and the Bornu-kanem Empires. Unfortunately today, almost all these empires and kingdoms has disappeared. The flourishing Trans-Saharan trades have also disappeared. The universities of Timbuctu and Sankore and other institutions were also destroyed.

REASONS FOR THE SATANIC RAGE AGAINST THE BLACK MAN

> *Why do the heathen rage, and the people imagine a vain thing? The kings of the earth set themselves, and the rulers take counsel together, against the LORD, and against his anointed, saying, (Psalm 2:1-2).*

The enemy does not oppose anything that does not pose a challenge to his kingdom. You do not waste your buckets on a corpse.

1. God is preparing Africa for the end time harvest of souls.

> *Princes shall come out of Egypt; Ethiopia shall soon stretch out her hand unto God (Psalm 68:31).*

> *Thus saith the LORD, The labour of Egypt, and merchandise of Ethiopia and of the Sabeans, men of stature, shall come over unto thee, and they shall be thine: they shall come after*

thee; in chains they shall come over, and they shall fall down unto thee, they shall make supplication unto thee, saying, Surely God is in thee; and there is none else, these is no God (Isa.45:14).

2. God has always used Africa to protect, support and provide for His move.

3. Africa shall become a spiritual military school in the last days from where soldiers of the cross shall be prepared and sent forth to all the nations of the world.

4. One may see the cycle of the spread of Christianity to Asia, Africa, Europe, America and back to Africa and the rest of the world. This cycle will repeat itself in the last days when Africans and Asians will take the gospel to Europe.

5. Africa represents the 'spiritual eyes' of the nations.

6. The Almighty has always relied on black people in times of crisis.

7. Whenever God wants to start a new move a black man has always come along.

No wonder there is a wicked satanic rage to stop the black man from fulfilling his divine purpose and destiny.

WHAT IS IT THAT HAS NOW DIVERTED US FROM THIS DIVINE PURPOSE?

What is it that has now diverted us from this divine purpose? Why has Africa now become a land of hewers of wood and drawers of water?

1. SIN, Particularly Idolatry

The first thing is sin. Sin will kill, and God hates sin with perfect hatred. As far as we continue in sin, we shall travel further and further from God's purpose. The sinner will become a slave, a hewer of wood and drawer of water.

An old woman told me a story that her grandfather was a village chief, who used to pound one day old babies in mortars, because he did not want to die on time. Sin has diverted the black man from where God wants him to be. As long as we continue on the pattern of sin as our forefathers did, then we remain in bondage. We need to get out of this fast.

The late White South African author, Alla Paton, sums it all up in 'Cry the beloved country'.

"One is inclined to weep at the number of educated people produced by the giant of Africa only for them to escape from hot and oppressive African governments in Africa to serve foreign powers. Those who chose to remain are either made sterile by bureaucracy or charmed

from producing their best by their less fortunate demon-possessed brethren."

Idolatry is at the root of the African problem, be it social or economic.

Today the whole of Africa is going through tough times because our ancestors had gone against the laws of the Almighty God. God did not give us wealth to revive our idols. Take the case of Nigeria celebrating the Festival of Arts and Culture in 1977. Many wellmeaning Nigerians spoke against the FESTAC. Late Chief Obafemi Awolowo in the Sunday Times of December 7th, 1975 said:

"I don't know what they stand to achieve by the cultural jamboree." In my view, it is unnecessary for the nation to revive every primitive culture for the people to see.

He said it would look as if we want to go backward simply because we don't know how to go forward. As for the white race he said:

"They are interested in watching us demonstrate our naivety and primitivity. What is necessary now is that we should continue to improve in technological know-how and not to be showing the world how primitive we are."

In his opinion, "the multi-million naira meant for FESTAC should be diverted to equipping our laboratories, expanding our educational facilities, improving agriculture, health and veterinary services.

"The nation would then gain a lot rather than watch primitive exhibitions."

Despite all the wise counsel, the Government went ahead and staged it.

Africa is like a caged champion. If the land and minerals are well managed, she can feed and finance the whole world.

2. DEMON WORSHIP

The demon worship. As long as we continue to worship idols, God will be far away from us. There are so many strange places around today where things that are not of God are worshiped. The black man unfortunately will still travel away far from where God wants him to be, because of this. All idols should be destroyed.

3. SACRIFICES TO DARK POWERS

Sacrifices to dark powers. This is one of the diversions taking us far away from God's purpose. We have heard testimonies of people kidnaped; what were the kidnappers going to do with the body? Sacrifice.

4. THE SPIRIT OF POLYGAMY

The spirit of polygamy. This has destroyed so many lives. Today, many so-called educated people are polygamists and have no qualms about it.

5. SEXUAL PERVERSION

Sexual perversion. This also has destroyed so many lives. A sister prayed, "O Lord, what has been holding me back?" God showed her a vision of ninety-two men and said, "you have slept with all these men." She said, "No, I have only one boy friend." Then an angel gave her this analysis; "Your boy friend has been sleeping with another girl. That makes two. The other person that the girl has been sleeping with, has had sex with five other men. These five other men, have slept with a total of twenty women, and some of them were prostitutes." By the time the angel finished calculating, the total number was ninety-two. This has destroyed many people beyond repair.

If you are reading this book and you are still traveling on this sinful road, I plead that you repent and change. A lot of useful people have been captured by strange women and this is paralyzing their lives and causing trouble. Foolish men will never learn.

When MFM was at her former place, in Old Yaba Road, Lagos, a woman came to me with one underwear. I asked, "What is it for?" She said, "When I was in the world, this is what we use to catch foolish men." I said, "what do you do?" She said, "we put it in the bottom of the pot, cook our stew in it and dish it to the man. Once he has eaten this 'pant soup', he is finished. If he has a wife at home, he will forget her." Perhaps you are reading this book and have eaten 'pant soup', God will deliver you. (Amen.)

6. DEAD CHURCHES

Dead churches. This is where people just go and practise a dead religion. So the devil has a good reason for destroying a lot of people who should be free from bondage. God wants you to be delivered. He wanted to lift up your head, break the fetters and set you free. We should go back to our position which God has given to us. We should stop hugging and kissing our bondage.

7. POLLUTED LAND

Our land is polluted. Most parts of our land are polluted and unless we redeem them, many problems will continue to rob us of our blessings. A lot of our land is in bondage with altars to evil things. We build good things on bad land. I do not know whether you have thought about all these things. Most of our land are prisons and local altars, where evil things have been done and demons are in charge. As long as we do not break this and redeem the land, we will still be struggling as a people.

Why does the black man pour libation on the ground? Why do they pour sand on where they say they have seen ghosts? Why do they remove sand from foot-prints? Why do herbalists pay homage to the ground? Why do black men swear by the earth? Why do people use the soil as charms? They know that there are certain powers that they have been using in the demonic world and these have been diverting things.

You are going to pray at this juncture.

"O Lord, deliver the black man from blindness."

In some places in Africa, you can still see some shrines, where people used to worship snakes. When you buy such a land and build your company or your house there, you have built on evil altars, so the demons will come in and start to cause confusion there. It is because of what I am telling you. Our land is polluted and filled with all kinds of demons.

There was a time we were praying with a girl who folded something in a black nylon bag, and said, "I want to hand this instrument over to you sir. It was given to me by demons from the sea." The thing was the head of a dead serpent with its mouth wide open. The serpent was dry and inside the mouth were grains of white sand, the kind you find at the sea side. I asked, "What is this?" She said, "With this, I can know what is happening any where in the whole world. I can know what any one is doing at any particular time. All I have to do, is talk to the sand." She then asked what I was going to do with it? I said, "I am going to burn it." She begged me not to burn it, because it took her thirteen years to get it. We poured kerosene on it and set it on fire but it refused to burn. We put other things yet, it refused to burn. Then we prayed and it started to burn and the girl cried. Our land is polluted.

The Bible says, "At the name of Jesus every knee should bow, of things in heaven, things on the earth, things underneath the earth," but the area underneath the earth is still not clear to many people. However, it was clear to the black men a long time ago. We need to pray about this.

Perhaps you noticed that, since your company got to a particular location it was not doing well, you might have built on an altar. I was praying for a man whose business was not doing well sometime ago and the Lord showed me a vision. Two pregnant women fought, killed themselves and were buried in the ground where the company was housed. No wonder, things never worked out for the company. But immediately the company moved out of that place, it started to do well.

8. FOUNDATIONAL POSSESSION BY DEMONS

Foundational possession by demons. A lot of people get possessed and are put under demonic bondage right from the womb of their parents. When the foundation of a person's life has already been possessed by the enemy, to get out of it could be something else.

This is why, if you see a Christian ministry in Africa which says that there is no such thing as deliverance, it is just a matter of time because they have not understood the play of the demons. Most of us here, perhaps the father and the mother were not born in herbalist homes; but some of us might have been born in herbalist homes, and it is naive to believe that such a thing will have no effect on us at all. Also, that all you have to do is get born again. No; getting born again only gives you the weapon to redeem yourself from that kind of bondage. You still have to set yourself free.

Many people are under what we call collective captivity. This is a bondage that people have not directly put themselves into. It is the trick that the devil has used against many people. Right from the foundation he sat on them. The ones he cannot get in the womb, he waits till the eighth day when the naming ceremony is being performed. Then, the witches and wizards will gather together and give the babies names which they have already manufactured from their kingdom. They will put all kinds of demonic materials into the mouth of each child and right from that moment, the child is polluted. The devil forgets about him and goes after another.

So if we will change our position, we still have to be more serious with our deliverance prayers for the black man. Perhaps you reading this book, your great-grandfather and your great grandmother were born in hospitals in England; if your grandparents and your parents were also born in hospitals in England, never came to this country, and do not have incisions on their bodies, then you are free.

When you sit down and think and know that you were born in Africa, then you have some battles to fight. This is how the devil has been operating - causing troubles from the foundation. When something is in the foundation, it is not as easy to get at as something that is on the surface. Look at the eight ways beloved, that the enemy has successfully used to divert the black man from his purpose; and the way out, is for those of us who are Christians to get ready for the battle to deliver our people.

If you try to save your country and it is difficult, then save your town. If you try to get your town out of bondage and it is difficult, try your street. If you try to get your street out of bondage, and it is difficult, try your household. If you try to get your household out of bondage and it is difficult, you had better deliver yourself. The situation is, Christian, set yourself free, after which you can help others.

INDIVIDUAL PURPOSE

Just as there is a general diversion, there are individual satanic diversions on peoples' lives too. A lot of people have placed the ladder of their lives on the wrong walls because they have been spiritually manipulated. Apart from this general thing, when you were created in the beginning, God had a programme, a divine purpose for your life. He did not call you here to be messing around, God has a divine destiny for you. It is wrong teaching and a very demonic doctrine for you to believe that if God has a good life for somebody, that whatever happens, the person will live that good life.

The fact that God says, "I will open the windows of heaven and there shall be blessings," does not mean that when the blessings arrive, the person will get them. They are two separate things. Try and understand this. The divine destiny for Jabez was not what was happening to him until he decided to change his life. He refused to be diverted.

Once God has a divine programme for your life and you refuse to move just a little bit to the right hand side, that is it. Forty days journey will become forty years. What should come easily will become very difficult and if the person is not careful, he will eventually end up in hell fire, because of this diversion. God has a purpose for your life, He has a programme for your life, He has what He wants you to be, He has the person He wants you to marry, the school He wants you to go, everything is there according to His plan.

Someone gave a testimony; the person was a big man with a big degree, but he was not making it. Then one day he prayed in anger and God directed him to a man of God who declared, "Mister, you are a big man, with a big degree, but all your 50 years or so, you have been pursuing shadows, and are not doing what God has designed for you originally." The man said, "What should Satanic Diversion of The Black Man 36 I do?" The man of God told him to go and pray. God then revealed to him that he was supposed to be selling vegetable oil. The man then obeyed and within a few months, he became a millionaire. That is what happens when you are within God's programme. If you are out, even by one foot, you will have problems.

A lot of people who are reading this book now have been diverted demonically. Some people have spent 50 or 40 years preparing firewood in dead churches. Some have spent a longer time than that cooking food for the enemy, carrying it to the sacrifice place or putting it at the doormat of the enemy. God has a divine purpose and a divine programme for you and until you locate it and begin to walk in it, there will continue to be trouble. You may think that all the witches in the country are against you whereas, all you need to do is go back to what God wants you to do. Not what you want to do but what He wants you to do.

I feel sorry for many sisters. God plants a very good husband somewhere and says, "this is your husband, he is staying there." But from no where, the devil is providing a diversion. The sister who is looking for a good husband is now going around with a married man; and since her hands are already full, God will say, "I cannot put two things in this hand, drop your diversion and get the correct husband." But people usually stick to the diversion, some for years, until the devil says, "yes, if you want, you can now go; I have already finished my assignment." I pray that such people will be delivered in Jesus' name.

HOW DO YOU KNOW THOSE WHO HAVE BEEN DIVERTED?

1. All efforts at moving ahead, ends in failure. This shows that there is a problem.

2. Always dreaming about your place of birth and returning to a particular location. Maybe you find yourself in the house you were living in when you were a child or in your former secondary school. God is telling you that you have been diverted at that age and you must come back. If the dream begins to repeat itself, God is telling you that you have not done anything about it, or that what you have done, is not good enough.

3. If you have ever been pursued by masquerades or serpents. Why are they pursuing you? They want you to miss your way. The person they are pursuing, cannot carefully look at where he is going. They just want the person to miss the way.

4. Blockages at the edge of miracles.

5. Perpetual restlessness in marriage. When people complain that there have been problems since they got married.

6. Inability to complete any good thing.

7. Constantly owing and never balanced financially.

8. Amputated breakthroughs.

9. Perpetual spiritual backwardness

10. Imaginary enemies.

11. Consistently making mistakes.

12. Women who are always sent packing, back to their family houses. What many people are calling our family house can be called a slaughter house.
13. Constant failures.
14. Seeing things which other people do not see.
15. Business failures, especially after moving into a new location.
16. Evil inheritance.

Sometimes, beloved, it is better for you to work with your own hands and accumulate your properties. When you do not know the origin of a wealth or a property, and someone wills it to you and you sit on it, you will share in its punishment.

A brother who was the only child of his mother inherited two houses from her. When those two houses got into his hands, his finances turned upside down. Before he had those two houses, he was doing well; he did not borrow, but immediately those two houses got into his hands, and rent from the houses began to enter into his account, trouble started. He prayed about this for five years. He did not know what was wrong. It got so bad that he could not feed himself properly.

Then one day he cried unto the Lord and asked what was happening? What has gone wrong? The Lord said, "why did you not ask me these past five years? You have an evil inheritance. Don't you know how your mother acquired these houses? She acquired them by burying cows, so you are sharing in her punishment." God then said that he should abandon the houses. The second week his fortune changed again and things began to work well for him. All those who are fighting for an inheritance, maybe God is even helping you, when you do not get a phase of it. Immediately you get your own share, another battle will start except the person who left the inheritance was a Christian before he died.

WHAT DO WE DO NOW?

You are going to pray. God brought this book to you for a purpose. Nobody is reading this book by accident. By your reading it, the devil has made another mistake. The devil can make mistakes. He did not read the Bible properly enough to find out that Jesus said, "If I be lifted up, I will draw all men onto me." He made a mistake and went to lift Jesus up on the cross and then what happened, He drew all men to Himself.

Because there is a general satanic diversion for the black race, the way out is to get back to God, repent and turn from our wicked ways. If we could come together to do this, the white man too would become our servants. If we repent, turn from our wicked ways, come before the Lord, stop depending on our local intelligence and depend on God, things will change for good.

The first step towards rejecting evil diversion is to be born again. Stop practising religion. Taste and see that the Lord is good.

1. You have to get born again.

2. You have to repent (both nationally and individually).
3. Then you renounce any known conscious or unconscious covenant.
4. You violently address the evil altar.
5. Then you paralyse the strong man.
6. Employ Biblical warfare strategies to obtain freedom.

This is how to get out of the diversion. If you are going to stay where your pastor is saying that there is no deliverance, may God have mercy on you. Jesus spent one-third of His time doing deliverance.

Let us see an example in the Bible which is a very good book. It is our manual. The Bible will tell you who your enemy is, the tactics of the enemy and how to defeat the enemy; how to get the aggressive angels of God to fight for you, and how to paralyse evil altars.

> ***1 Kings 13:1-5: And, behold, there came a man of God out of Judah by the word of the LORD unto Bethel: and Jeroboam stood by the altar to burn incense. And he cried against the altar in the word of the LORD, and said, O altar, altar, thus saith the LORD; Behold, a child shall be born unto the house of David, Josiah by name; and upon thee shall he offer the priests of the high places that burn incense upon thee, and men's bones shall be burnt upon thee. And he gave a sign the same day, saying, This is the sign which the LORD hath spoken; Behold, the altar shall be rent, and the ashes that are upon it shall be poured***

> ***out. And it came to pass, when king Jeroboam heard the saying of the man of God, which had cried against the altar in Bethel, that he put forth his hand from the altar, saying, Lay hold on him. And his hand, which he put forth against him, dried up, so that he could not pull it in again to him. The altar also was rent, and the ashes poured out from the altar, according to the sign which the man of God had given by the word of the LORD.***

This man of God came out of Judah and stood where the king was burning incense. Human beings were standing around but it was the altar that God sent this man to address. There is a demon inside this altar, who will hear what God had to say. So he cried against the altar. The Bible says, "The Lord is a man of war, the Lord is His name."

Any evil hand pointed against you will dry up in Jesus' name.

We have to paralyse every evil altar and every prophet or priest of the altar who wants to harass you for pulling down the altar. Their hands will dry up if they raise them against you. Many materials from people are taken to evil altars everyday. Pictures, shoes, clothes etc. are used to attack people with a view to sacrificing them on the altar of the dead.

All the prayer points must be said with holy anger. If the enemy diverts you for just one second, that one second can have a life time implication. It can affect your life for ever. We thank God for one thing; He is the only person who can re-organise a diversion, no matter how crooked it is to a divine appointment. Cry unto him with an open heart; with a heart filled with righteous anger. We use holy anger when the enemy is going beyond his boundary.

Some of us do not understand that one simple careless immorality can change the course of one's life. One small herb that you take from someone and put in your mouth can change the course of your life. The devil is not a fool, he is very crafty. If he can succeed in diverting a person and leave him to be floating around, he is contented. He knows that the person will soon float back to him, because he is traveling on a journey that is not divinely prescribed. Beloved, I want us to pray these prayer points seriously.

PRAYER SECTION

1. I recover my steps from every evil diversion, in the name of Jesus.

2. I recover my steps from every satanic diversion, in the name of Jesus.

3. I reject every satanic diversion in the name of Jesus.

4. Every evil altar fashioned against me, be roasted, in the name of Jesus

5. Every enemy of peace in this continent, receive double frustration, in the name of Jesus.

6. We bind every blood drinking demon in this country, in the name of Jesus.

7. I cover myself and my family with the fire of God's protection, in the name of Jesus.

PRAYER STRATEGY TO FRUSTRATE SATANIC DIVERSION

African Christians will have to work harder than we are presently doing if we are to redeem our land and frustrate satanic diversion. To redeem our continent we must:

1. Locate and inspect areas where satan has imprisoned the continent.

2. Take steps to completely remove our continent from satan's power.

3. Hold up the redemptive power of the blood of Jesus over the continent.

4. Pray for restoration of the continent to divine standard.

In order to do all these, the following steps are recommended:

1. Those with the burden should share it with others.

2. Secure the participation of Christians who are courageous, holy, faith-filled and who are intercessors.

3. Prepare your heart through repentance, humility, holiness, prayer and fasting.

4. Travail in prayer and engage in prayer-warfare until God's purposes are fulfilled. The prayer sections could follow the guidelines below:

   a) Praise worship.

   b) Confession of sin to the Lord on-behalf of our people, particularly the ancestors.

   c) Cover yourself with the blood of Jesus.

   d) Ask God to send protecting angels to camp around you.

   e) Renunciation of covenant.

f) Paralyzing the ancestral strongman.

g) Pray aggressive bondage-breaking prayers.

h) Locate areas of demonic operations, like shrines, crossroads, beaches, evil forests, palaces, market places, etc and attack these strongholds with prayers.

i) Pray violent prayers to address and disgrace evil altars on high places, residents god/gods/idols, pollution of land with blood, demonic religions of the founders and original settlers, evil foundations, covenanted seat of power and evil thrones.

j) Pray to release and recover lost benefits and blessings.

k) Prophesy life and blessing on the continent.

5. Believers should engage in aggressive evangelism to turn our nations to Christ.

6. Sample prayer points are listed in English and French at the back of this booklet.

PRAYERS FOR AFRICA

ENGLISH

SCRIPTURES: 1 Tim. 2:1-2: I exhort therefore, that, first of all, supplications, prayers, intercessions, and giving of thanks, be made for all men; For kings, and for all that are in authority; that we may lead a quite and peaceable life in all godliness and honesty.

Jer. 1:10: See, I have this day set thee over the nations and over the kingdoms, to root out, and to pull down, and to destroy, and to throw down, to build, and to plant.

Isa. 61:1-6, Eph. 6:10-16.

1. Father, in the name of Jesus, we confess all the sins and iniquities of the land, of our ancestors, of our leaders, and of the people. E.g., violence, rejection of God, corruption, idolatries, robbery, suspicion, injustice, bitterness, bloodyriots, pogroms, rebellion, conspiracy, shedding of innocent blood, tribal conflicts, child-kidnaping and murder, occultism, mis-management, negligence, etc.

2. We plead for mercy and forgiveness, in the name of Jesus.

3. O Lord, remember our land and redeem our land.

4. O Lord, save our land from destruction and judgement.

5. Let Your healing power begin to operate upon our land, in Jesus' name.

6. Let all forces of darkness hindering the move of God in this nation be rendered impotent, in the name of Jesus.

7. We command the spiritual strongman in charge of this country to be bound and be disgraced, in the name of Jesus.

8. Let every evil establishment and satanic tress in Africa be uprooted and cast into fire, in the name of Jesus.

9. We come against every spirit of the anti-Christ working against Africa and we command them to be permanently frustrated, in the name of Jesus.

10. We command the stones of fire from God, to fall upon every continental satanic operation and activities, in the name of Jesus.

11. Let the desire, plans, devices and expectations of the enemy for Africa be completely frustrated, in the name of Jesus.

12. Let every satanic curse on Africa fall down to the ground and die, in the name of Jesus.

13. By the blood of Jesus, let all sins, ungodliness, idolatry and all vices cease in the land, in the name of Jesus.

14. We break every evil covenant and dedications made upon our land, in the name of Jesus.

15. We plead the blood of Jesus over Africa, in the name of Jesus.

16. We decree the will of God for this land, whether the devil likes it or not, in the name of Jesus.

17. Let all contrary powers and authorities in Africa be confounded and be put to shame, in the name of Jesus.

18. We close every satanic gate in every nation of this continent, in Jesus' name.

19. Let every evil throne in Africa be dashed to pieces, in the name of Jesus.

20. We bind all negative forces operating in the lives of our leaders in Africa, in the name of Jesus.

21. O Lord, lay Your hands of fire and power upon all our leaders in Africa, in the name of Jesus.

22. We bind every blood-drinking demon in Africa, in Jesus' name.

23. Let the Prince of Peace reign in every department of Africa, in the name of Jesus.

24. Let every anti-Gospel spirit be frustrated and be rendered impotent, in the name of Jesus.

25. O Lord, give leaders in Africa, who will see their roles as a calling instead of an opportunity to amass wealth.

26. Let all forms of ungodliness be destroyed by the divine fire of burning, in the name of Jesus.

27. O Lord, let our leaders in Africa be filled with divine understanding and wisdom.

28. O Lord, let our leaders in Africa follow the counsel of God and not of man and demons.

29. O Lord, let our leaders in Africa have wisdom and knowledge of God.

30. O Lord, let our government be the kind that would obtain direction and leading of God.

31. Let every satanic altar in Africa receive the fire of God and be burned to ashes, in the name of Jesus.

32. We silence every satanic prophet, priest and practitioners in the mighty name of Jesus. We forbid them from interfering in the affairs of Africa, in the name of Jesus.

33. Let the blood of Jesus cleanse our land from every blood pollution, in the name of Jesus.

34. We command the fire of God on all idols, sacrifices, rituals, shrines and local satanic thrones in Africa, in the name of Jesus.

35. We break any conscious and unconscious agreement made between the people of Africa and satan, in the name of Jesus.

36. We dedicate and claim all our cities for Jesus, in the name of Jesus.

37. Let the blessings and presence of the Lord be experienced in all our cities, in the name of Jesus.

38. We decree total paralysis on lawlessness, immorality and drug addiction in Africa, in the name of Jesus.

39. Let the power, love and glory of God be established in our land, in the name of Jesus.

40. Let there be a thirst and hunger for God in the hearts of Christians of this nation, in the name of Jesus.

41. O Lord, deposit the spirit of revival in Africa.

42. O Lord, lay Your hands of power and might upon the Armed Forces and Police, Establishments and Institutions, Universities and Colleges of Africa.

43. Let the resurrection power of the Lord Jesus Christ fall upon our economy in Africa, in the name of Jesus.

44. Let there be fruitfulness and prosperity in every area of Africa, in the name of Jesus.

45. We command every threat to the political, economic and social stability in the land to be paralyzed, in the name of Jesus.

46. We frustrate every satanic external influences by other nations, in the name of Jesus.

47. We command confusion and disagreement between the sons of the bondwoman planning to cage the nation, in the name of Jesus.

48. We break any covenant between any satanic external influence and our leaders, in the name of Jesus.

49. We paralyse every spirit of wastage of economic resources in Africa, in the name of Jesus.

50. Let the sprit of borrowing depart completely from Africa, in the name of Jesus.

51. O Lord, show Yourself mighty in the affairs of Africa.

52. Let the Kingdom of Christ come into Africa, in the name of Jesus.

53. O Lord, do new things in Africa to show Your power and greatness to the heathen.

54. Let the Kingdom of our Lord Jesus Christ come into the heart of every person in Africa, in the name of Jesus.

55. O Lord, have mercy upon Africa.

56. Let all the glory of Africa that has departed be restored, in the name of Jesus.

57. Let all un-evangelized areas of Africa be reached with the Gospel of our Lord Jesus Christ, in the name of Jesus.

58. O Lord, send forth labourers into Your vineyard to reach the unreached in Africa.

59. We dismantle the stronghold of poverty in Africa, in the name of Jesus.

60. O Lord, install Your agenda for Africa.

61. Let every power of darkness operating in our educational institution be disgraced, in the name of Jesus.

62. Let the satanic representatives of key posts in Africa be dismantled, in the name of Jesus.

63. Let every evil spiritual throne behind all physical thrones in Africa be dismantled, in the name of Jesus.

64. Let every satanic covenant made on behalf of Africa by anyone be nullified, in the name of Jesus.

65. We trample upon the serpents and scorpions of ethnic clashes in Africa, in the name of Jesus.

66. We decree a re-alignment of situation around us to favour us in Africa, in the name of Jesus.

67. We dethrone every strange king installed in the spirit upon us in African, in the name of Jesus.

68. Let all principalities, powers, rulers of darkness and spiritual wickedness in heavenly places militating against Africa be bound and disgraced, in the name of Jesus.

69. Let righteousness reign in every part of Africa, in the name of Jesus.

70. Praises.

FRENCH

LES ECRITURES SAINTES: ***1Tim. 2:1-2: J'exhorte donc, avant toutes choses, à faire des prières, des supplications, des requêtes, des actions de grâces, pour tous les hommes, pour les rois et pour tous ceux qui sont élevés en dignité, afin que nous menions une vie paisible et tranquille, en toute piété et honnêteté.***

Jer. 1: 10: Regarde, je t'établis aujourd'hui sur les nations et sur les royaumes, pour que tu arraches et que tu abattes, pour que tu ruines et que tu détruises, pour que tu bâtisses et que tu plantes.

Esaie 61: 1-6; Eph. 6:10-16.

1. Père Céleste, au nom de Jésus, nous confessons tous les pêchés et les iniquités de la terre de nos ancêtres, de nos leaders et du peuple: par exemple, la violence, le rejet de Dieu, la corruption, les idolâtries, le vol, le soupçon, l'injustice, l'amertume, les émeutes sanguines, les pogroms, la révolte, la conspiration, faire couler le sang des innocents, les conflits entre tribus, l'enlèvement des enfants et meurtre, l'occultisme, la mauvaise administration, la négligence etc.

2. Nous implorons ta miséricorde et ton pardon, au nom de Jésus.

3. Seigneur, souviens-toi de notre continent et rachète notre terre.

4. Seigneur, sauve notre continent de la destruction et du jugement.

5. Que ton pouvoir de guérir, de soulager commence par opérer sur notre continent, au nom de Jésus.

6. Que toutes les forces des ténèbres empêchant Dieu d'agir dans le continent, deviennent faibles ou impotentes, au nom de Jésus.

7. Nous ordonnons l'homme fort spirituel en charge de ce continent d'être ligoté et honni, au nom de Jésus.

8. Que tous les établissements maléfiques et toutes les plantations des arbres diaboliques en Afrique soient déracinés et jetés au feu, au nom de Jésus.

9. Nous sommes contre tout esprit de l'anti-Christ en fonction contre ce continent et nous l'ordonnons d'être frustré d'une maniere permanente, au nom de Jésus.

10. Nous commandons les pierres de feu de l'Eternel d'abattre toutes les machinations sataniques érigées dans le continent, au nom de Jésus.

11. Que tout désir, projet, mécanisme et espoir de l'ennemi contre ce continent soient complètement frustrés, au nom de Jésus.

12. Que toutes les malédictions diaboliques sur ce continent s'écrasent et meurent, au nom de Jésus.

13. Par le Sang de Jésus que tous les péchés, impiété, idolâtrie et vices cessent dans le continent, au nom de Jésus.

14. Nous détruisons tout engagement maléfique et toute consécration dirigés ou entrepris contre ce continent, au nom de Jésus.

15. Nous implorons le Sang de Jésus sur ce continent, au nom de Jésus.

16. Nous décrétons la volonté de Dieu pour l'Afrique que le diable veuille ou pas, au nom de Jésus.

17. Que toute puissance et autorité contraires à notre continent soient confuses et honnies, au nom de Jésus.

18. Nous fermons tout portail satanique dans chaque village ou ville de ce continent, au nom de Jésus.

19. Que tout trône maléfique en Afrique s'écrase, au nom de Jésus.

20. Nous ligotons toutes les forces contraires, en fonction dans la vie de nos leaders en Afrique, au nom de Jésus.

21. O Seigneur, mets tes mains de feu et de pouvoir sur tous nos leaders en Afrique, au nom de Jésus.

22. Nous ligotons tout diable buveur du sang en Afrique, au nom de Jésus.

23. Que le Prince de la paix règne dans tous les aspects de la vie de ce continent, au nom de Jésus.

24. Que tout esprit anti-évangile soit frustré et rendu impuissant, au nom de Jésus.

25. O Seigneur, donne-nous en Afrique des leaders qui verront leurs rôles comme une vocation et un appel au service, au lieu d'une occasion pour s'amasser des richesses.

26. Que toute forme d'impiété soit détruite par le divin feu ardent, au nom de Jésus.

27. O Seigneur, fais que nos leaders soient pleins d'intelligence et de sagesse.

28. O Seigneur, fais que les leaders d'Afrique suivent les conseils de l'Eternel et non ceux de l'homme ou du diable.

29. O Seigneur, fais que les leaders d'Afrique aient la sagesse et la connaissance de Dieu.

30. O Seigneur, fais que notre gouvernement soit celui qui obtient les instructions et les principes de Dieu.

31. Que tout autel démoniaque d'Afrique recoive le feu divin et soit rendu en cendres, au nom de Jésus.

32. Nous réduisons au silence tous les prophètes et les prêtres diaboliques ainsi que les féticheurs, au puissant nom de Jésus. Nous les interdisons de se mêler des affaires de cette nation.

33. Que le Sang de Jésus purifie notre terre de toute contamination sanguine, au nom de Jésus.

34. Nous ordonnons le feu de Dieu sur toutes les idoles, les sacrifices, les rituels, les hauts- lieux et les trônes sataniqués dans en Afrique, au nom de Jésus.

35. Nous brisons tout accord ou tout contact établi consciemment ou inconsciemment entre le peuple de l'Afrique et le diable, au nom de Jésus.

36. Nous revendiquons et consacrons toutes nos villes à Jésus, au nom de Jésus.

37. Que tout le monde éprouve la bénédiction et la présence de Dieu dans toutes nos villes et villages, au nom de Jésus.

38. Nous décrétons la paralysie totale sur toute anarchie, toute immoralité, toute addiction à la drogue dans en Afrique, au nom de Jésus.

39. Que la puissance, l'amour et la gloire de Dieu soient établis dans notre pays, au nom de Jésus.

40. Que les coeurs des chrétiens dans en Afrique aient soif et faim de Dieu, au nom de Jésus.

41. O Seigneur, dépose l'esprit de réveil spirituel dans ce continent.

42. O Seigneur, mets tes mains de pouvoir et de puissance sur l'Armée, la Police, les Etablissements et les Institutions, les Universités et Collèges de l'Afrique.

43. Que la puissance de la résurrection de Notre Seigneur Jésus Christ soit sur notre économie en Afrique, au nom de Jésus.

44. Que l'abondance et la prospérité soient dans les domaines de l'Afrique, au nom de Jésus.

45. Nous commandons que toute menace à la stabilité politique, économique et sociale en Afrique soit paralysée, au nom de Jésus.

46. Nous frustrons toutes les influences externes sataniques venant des autres nations, au nom de Jésus.

47. Nous ordonnons confusion et désaccord entre les fils de l'esclave qui cherchent à mettre en Afrique ou cette nation en cage, au nom de Jésus.

48. Nous brisons tout engagement entre toute influence externe diabolique et nos leaders, au nom de Jésus.

49. Nous paralysons tout esprit de gaspillage des ressources économiques en Afrique, au nom de Jésus.

50. Que l'esprit d'emprunter quitte complètement en Afrique, au nom de Jésus.

51. O Seigneur, démontre que tu es le tout PUISSANT dans les affaires de ce continent.

52. Que le royaume du CHRIST vienne dans ce continent, au nom de Jésus.

53. O Seigneur, fais des merveilles dans notre pays pour montrer ta PUISSANCE et ta GRANDEUR aux païens.

54. Que le royaume de Notre Seigneur Jésus vienne dans le coeur de chaque citoyen d'Afrique, au nom de Jésus.

55. O Seigneur, aie pitié de en Afrique.

56. Que toute la gloire de ce continent qui l'a quittée lui soit restaurée, au nom de Jésus.

57. Que tout domaine non évangélisé d'Afrique soit atteint par la Bonne Nouvelle de Notre Seigneur Jésus-Christ, au nom de Jésus.

58. O Seigneur, envoie des ouvriers dans Ton vignoble pour atteindre les inaccessibles dans en Afrique.

59. Nous démantelons la forteresse de pauvreté dans ce continent, au nom de Jésus.

60. O Seigneur, installe ton programme pour ce continent.

61. Que toute puissance des ténèbres en fonction dans nos établissements scolaires soit honnie, au nom de Jésus.

62. Que tous les représentatifs diaboliques de postes importants en Afrique soient déchus, au nom de Jésus.

63. Que tout trône spirituel derrière ou supportant tous les trônes physiques en Afrique soit démantelé, au nom de Jésus.

64. Que tout engagement diabolique fait en compte en Afrique par quiconque soit nullifié, au nom de Jésus.

65. Nous foulons au pied tous les serpents et les scorpions des conflits ethniques en Afrique, au nom de Jésus.

66. Nous décrétons les réalignements des situations autour de nous en notre faveur, au nom de Jésus.

67. Nous détrônons tout roi étrange installé sur nous dans le domaine spirituel en Afrique, au nom de Jésus.

68. Que toutes les principautés, les puissances, les souverains des ténèbres, la méchanceté spirituelle dans les lieux célestes militant contre ce continent soient ligotés et honnis, au nom de Jésus.

69. Que la droiture ou la vertu règne dans tous les systèmes de ce continent, au nom de Jésus.

70. Actions de grâce - Louanges.

MFM and The Author

Dr.D.K. Olukoya is the General Overseer of the Mountain of Fire and Miracles Ministries and The Battle Cry Christian Ministries.

The Mountain of Fire and Miracles Ministries Headquarters is the largest single Christian congregation in Africa with attendance of over 120,000 in single meetings.

MFM is a full gospel ministry devoted to the revival of Apostolic signs, Holy Ghost Fireworks, miracles and the unlimited demonstration of the power of God to deliver to the uttermost. Absolute holiness within and without as spiritual insecticide and pre-requisite for heaven is openly taught.

MFM is a do-it-yourself Gospel Ministry, where your hands are trained to wage war and your fingers to do battles.
Dr. Olukoya holds a first class honours degree in Micro-biology from the University of Lagos and a PhD in Molecular Genetics from the University of Reading, United Kingdom. As a researcher, he has over seventy scientific publications to his credit.

Anointed by God. Dr. Olukoya is a prophet, evangelist, teacher and preacher of the Word. His life and that of his wife, Shade and their son Elijah Toluwani are living proofs that all power belongs to God.

ISBN 978-2947-15-6

Printed in Great Britain
by Amazon

38684951R00040